written by:
# Kathy Glover

illustrations by:
# Rachelle Houchin

© 2013 Rachelle Houchin and Kathlyn Glover

All Rights Reserved

ISBN:  978-0-615-85682-7

Published by:  Kathlyn Glover
                    kathlyn.glover@gmail.com
                    www.LoveTheBabies.com

2

There's a place in California
Where the hillsides meet the sea.
You could say the beauty is
As lovely as can be.

High above the ocean
Live a family and their dog.
The yard is full with flowers and trees,
The birds sing their sweet songs.

Her family calls her Poko,
She frolics in the sun.
Happy in their company,
She likes to jump and run.

4

Usually in the evening,
Poko's family takes a walk.
With the other plants and animals
she sometimes stops and talks.

One evening while out walking,
A pinecone Poko met.
The pinecone called hello to her,
She stopped to sniff its scent.

"Hi, I'm Poko!" was the greeting,
With a smile upon her face.
In the wheel of life connection,
Waves of love engulfed the space.

5

"Sweet Poko," said her pinecone friend,
"I'm fearful for my life.
There's danger here beside the street,
My heart is torn with strife.

"Poko, will you help me please?
It shouldn't take too long.
Take me to the forest green,
Where I can grow up strong."

Poko listened as her owner
Gently tugged upon the leash.
"I'll be back for you," she said,
"Yes, I'll be back indeed."

8

Around the corner in the dusk,
Poko walked away.
The pinecone sighed but still she felt
The magic of this day.

10

Poko rested in her home,
Her owner stroked her fur.
In awhile she got up quietly
And waited by the door.

12

"**D**on't be long," the tall girl said,
And stroked behind her ears.
Poko walked into the night -
Her purpose was quite clear.

Outside she changed her senses,
Her nose became her guide.
She was surrounded by the darkness
And the smells and sounds of night.

14

Poko raced across the yard,
She knew she was on track.
A car roared by and startled her,
Branches scraped her back!

Around the corner Poko ran
Her nose close to the ground.
She saw the pinecone on the street -
She felt her heartbeat pound.

16

She reached her friend and nuzzled her
So gently with her nose.
"You made it!" said the pinecone,
"Now, it's time for us to go!"

Poko very gently held
The pinecone in her mouth.
She started out, but with a thought,
Decided to sit down.

18

"Are you sure you want to leave?"
Poko asked her friend.
"It's not too late to call it off,
Just stay right here instead."

The pinecone sighed with Poko's words,
Her heart began to sink.
"Let me tell you what I know,
Then tell me what you think.

"It's from the forest they got my mom
When she was but a seedling.
This place lived in her memory,
Her heart still held this feeling.

"She wished for me that I could live
In the forest by the sea.
I'm a little scared but I want to know
How such a place might be.

"So c'mon my friend, get on the path!
Your nose will be our guide.
With our hearts, the stars and the smell of the sea,
We're in for a wild night's ride!"

19

20

Poko perked up her ears, put her nose to the ground,
And followed an ancient knowing.
The scent of the sea came in with the wind
As a guide to the place they were going.

Across cool watered lawns and dangerous streets
The pair carefully made their way.
They arrived at the forest just at the time
Of the dawning of the day.

22

The forest stood silent in the light of the dawn -
They could hear the crash of the waves.
Poko stepped in on the soft needle floor,
On the tall trees she felt herself gaze.

"Just put me right here," the pinecone said.
Poko gently put her down.
To the trees in the forest Poko announced,
"I return to you one of your own."

"We love you dear Poko," the forest trees said,
"What a wonderful friend you are!
To give yourself in service to others,
Is the greatest gift, by far."

24

"I've got to be going," Poko said to the trees,
To her friend gave one final soft nuzzle.
"The family I love will be missing me now,
They'll be worried and very puzzled."

Across glistening lawns and brightening streets,
Poko made her way quickly home.
She knew she felt different after this trip -
Her fears and her doubts were gone.

When Poko arrived she barked at the door,
"Poko's back!" came the cry filled with love.
She had hugs, a small scolding and petting galore,
The sun shone warm from above.


The seasons changed as all things do,
And time passed quickly by.
Flowers bloomed, birds flew south,
Clouds floated in the sky.

28

One morning while Poko played in the yard,
She heard her family say:
"Come on!  Let's go!  Hop in the car!
Let's go for a ride today!"

They drove in the car past the houses and yards,
Past a cat that ran into the brush.
With her face in the wind and her ears flying back,
The memory came in with a rush.

As they drew near the sea, with her sensitive ears,
Poko heard the crash of the waves.
In her mind was the thought of the night
When she and the pinecone were so brave.

30

They arrived at the sea and Poko jumped out;
She ran to the forest edge.
Filled with excitement, wonder and love,
The memories filled her head.

The forest was quiet as Poko walked in,
"Hi, it's Poko!" she said to her friends.
"I came back here with my family this time!
I'm so happy to see you again!"

32

"Hi Poko!" they said, "The pinecone is growing.
She's right over there in the sun."
"Hey Poko!" she heard, and she spied her old friend,
"Life in the forest is fun!"

34

Poko nuzzled the seedling and said with a smile,
"You've grown tall so quickly, I see.
You're living the life you wished you could live,
Here in the forest so green."

"Poko, it's you!" the pinecone said,
"I've thought of you most days.
My heart is full with gratitude
For the kindness that you gave.

"My forest family has loved me well,
They have made me feel so welcome.
It's because of you that I now know
The dream I had of home."

36

"Come on, let's go!" Poko's family called out.
She turned to look at her friend.
"You'll be in my heart, keep growing, stay strong!
It all works out in the end."


The End


........... of this adventure

www.ingramcontent.com/pod-product-compliance
Lightning Source LLC
Chambersburg PA
CBHW042156030726
47599CB00004B/750